FORENSICS
CHEMISTRY
AND CRIME

Sarah Jane Brian

TABLE OF CONTENTS

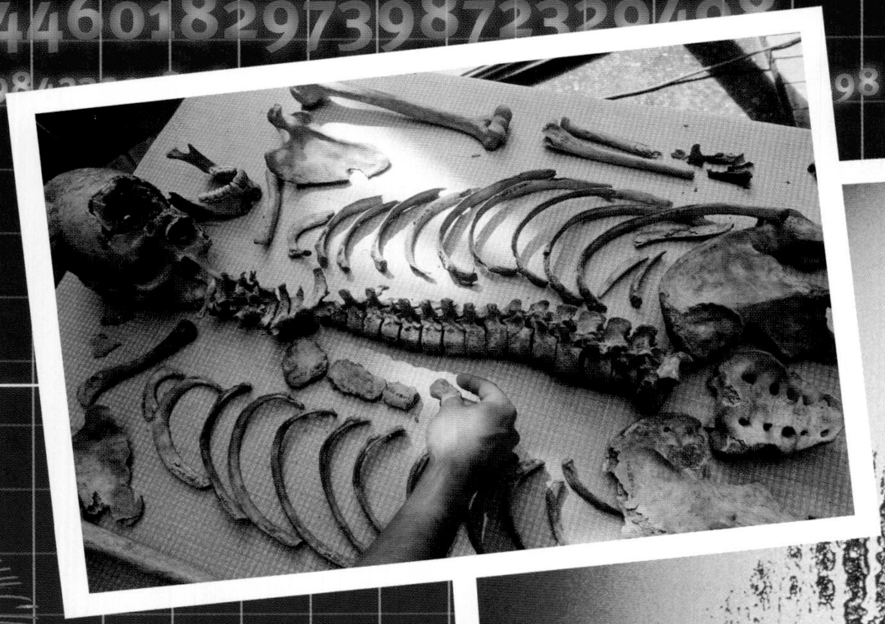

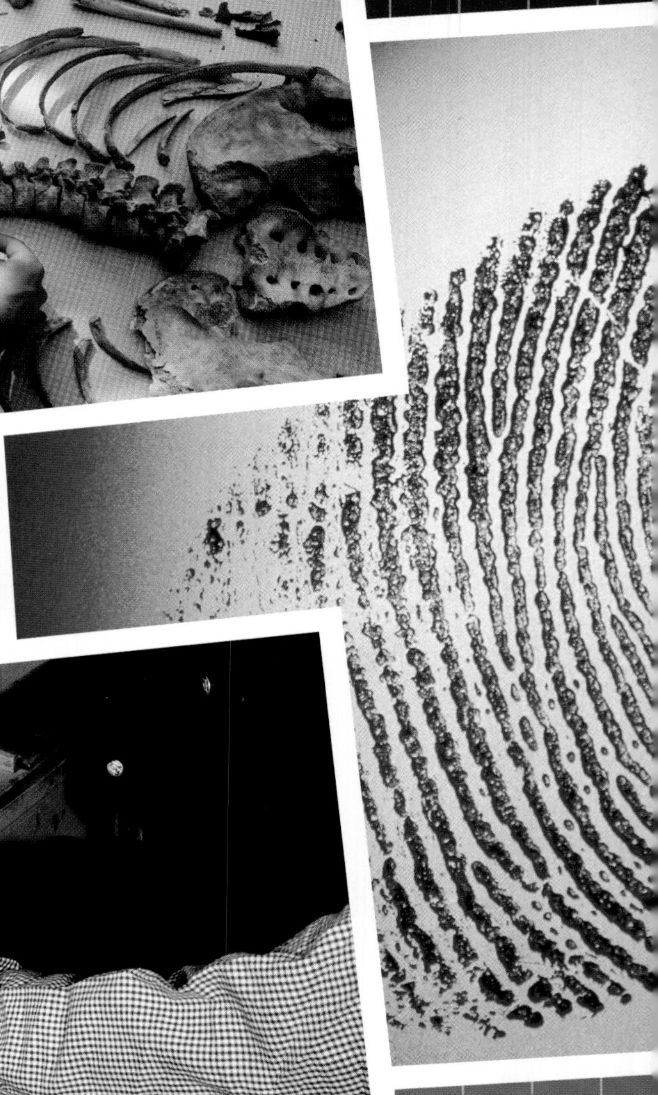

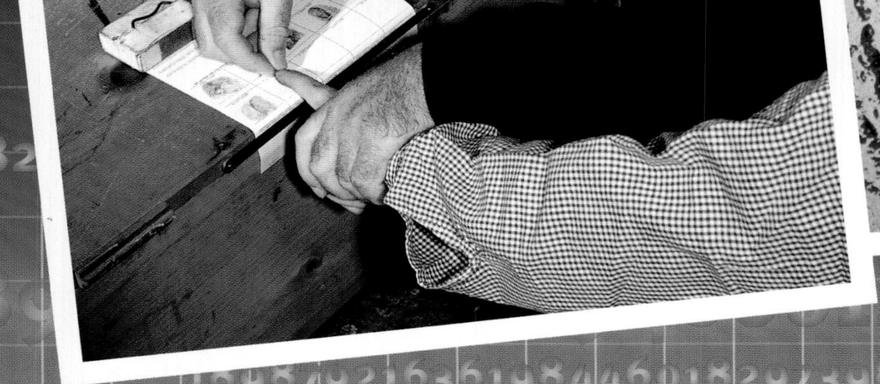

CRIME SCENE DO NOT ENTER

Words To Think About

Characteristics

found at crime scene

can be very tiny

?

trace evidence

What do you think the term **trace evidence** means?

Examples

drop of blood

fiber from clothing

?

casting

What do you think the word **casting** means in this book?

Meaning 1
throwing a fishing line (verb)

Meaning 2
finding actors for a play or movie (verb)

Meaning 3
a form made by pouring plaster into a mold (noun)

iii

Read for More Clues
ballistics,   page 22
casting,   page 21
trace evidence, page 3

ballistics

What do you think the word **ballistics** means?

Who are **ballistics** experts?

What do **ballistics** experts study?

scientists	?	police

gun barrels	?	bullet holes

iv

INTRODUCTION

A burglar sneaks up to a dark house. The burglar makes shoe prints in the mud. He breaks a window. As he climbs inside, he grabs the ledge. He leaves **fingerprints** (FIN-ger-prints). He cuts his hand on the broken glass. Drops of blood fall to the floor.

Shoe prints and fingerprints are clues. Broken glass and blood are also clues. **Forensic science** (fuh-REN-zik SY-ens) is the study of clues. Forensic experts use science to solve crimes.

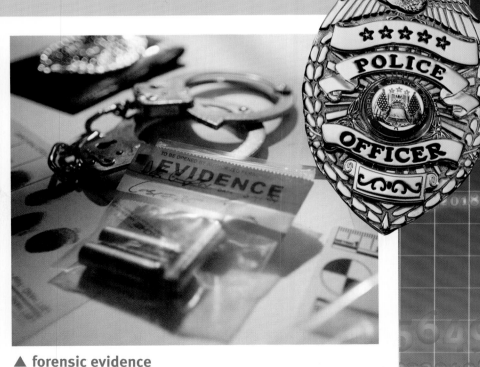

▲ forensic evidence

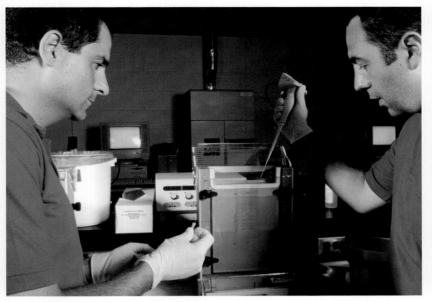

▲ These forensic scientists are studying DNA.

THE SCIENCE OF CRIME FIGHTING

Before the 1880s, police did not use science. Today, science helps solve crimes.

In this book, you will learn about many types of forensic science. First, see how science is used to find and study fingerprints. Next, read about **trace evidence** (TRASE EH-vih-dens). You will see how bones, **tool marks** (TOOL MARKS), and weapons help solve crimes.

Then, learn about **DNA** (DEE-EN-AY). DNA is in cells. Scientists take DNA from tiny bits of blood or saliva. They use DNA to find out who was at a crime scene.

Read on. Learn all about forensic science.

FINGERPRINTS

Look closely at your fingertips. Do you see the tiny ridges swirling around? Those are your fingerprints. All humans have fingerprints. In fact, we need them. They help us grip things. Without them, things would slip through our fingers.

NO TWO PRINTS ARE THE SAME

Police use fingerprints to identify (i-DEN-tih-fy) people. No two fingerprints are alike. Everyone has different fingerprints. Fingerprints do not change. They stay the same from birth to death.

It's a Fact

Everyone has his or her own unique fingerprints—even identical twins!

4

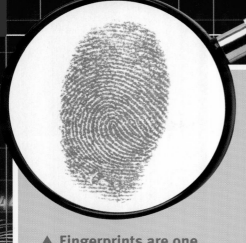

▲ Fingerprints are one of the best ways to identify someone.

with the same pattern. You might have a scar on one of your fingertips. But the scar can help police prove that a fingerprint is yours.

Have you ever looked at the bottoms of your feet? Footprints and fingerprints are alike. But most people wear shoes. Footprints are rarely found at crime scenes.

Some people try to remove their fingerprints. But fingerprints grow back

▲ Police rarely find bare footprints, but they often find shoe or boot prints.

FINGERPRINTS ARE EVERYWHERE

You have oils in your skin. You make fingerprints every time you touch something smooth. Touch a table, glass, or paper. Even if you just washed your hands, the oils leave a mark. Try pressing your fingertip on a mirror. You can see your fingerprint.

Criminals often leave fingerprints at the scene of a crime. Forensic scientists can use the prints to help solve the case.

▲ Usually, people are not even aware that they have left fingerprints behind.

In 1882, Alphonse Bertillon had an idea. He wanted to use science to keep track of criminals. His idea was to measure their heads, fingers, and bodies. He thought that no two people would have the same measurements.

Police measured each criminal they arrested. They checked their records to find a match. If they found one, they assumed the criminal had been in jail before.

In 1903, two men named Will West were put in the same jail. They had the same measurements! This showed that Bertillon's system didn't always work. But his ideas paved the way for the system we use today—fingerprints.

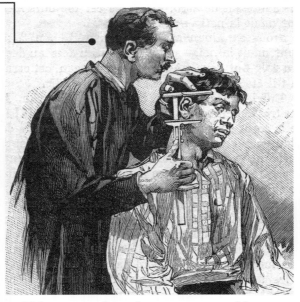

▲ This engraving shows a man taking measurements of a criminal's ear using Bertillon's system.

PATENT PRINTS AND LATENT PRINTS

Police look for fingerprints at crime scenes. Patent (PAY-tent) fingerprints are easy to see. A dirty hand leaves dark fingerprints. You can see the prints without any special tools.

Latent (LAY-tent) fingerprints are difficult to see. Police must use tools to see them. One tool is a special light.

▲ This is an example of a patent fingerprint.

FINGERPRINTS THROUGH HISTORY FI

Before Written History	Artists mark clay pots with fingerprints.	
1000 B.C.E.	In China, people use fingerprints to sign their names.	
1858	Sir William Herschel starts to study fingerprints. He learns that his own prints do not change after fifty years.	
1880	Dr. Henry Faulds says that fingerprints can be used to identify people. He finds that dusting with powder helps to see invisible prints.	
1892	Detectives use fingerprints to solve a case for the first time. The case takes place in Argentina.	
1999	The FBI creates a new computer system. It can store the fingerprints of 65 million people!	

GATHERING FINGERPRINT EVIDENCE

Police also use a powder to find latent fingerprints. Police may dust objects with this powder. The powder sticks to the oils that made the prints. Then police take photographs of the prints. Police may also use sticky tape to lift up powdered prints. Then they take the prints to a laboratory.

▲ Dusting for fingerprints may help police make an arrest.

EVERYDAY SCIENCE

All fingerprints are different, but most fall into one of three patterns. They are the whorl, the arch, and the loop. Look at the picture of each pattern. Which one looks the most like your fingerprints?

▲ whorl

▲ arch

▲ loop

MATCHING A PRINT

After police find a fingerprint, they try to match it to a person. An expert must find out who made the print.

Police may have a suspect, or person who they think is guilty. The expert compares the suspect's prints to the prints police found.

An expert may also use a computer. The computer holds pictures of millions of fingerprints.

The computer quickly searches for prints that might match. Then the expert carefully compares each print. The expert sees if the prints match anyone.

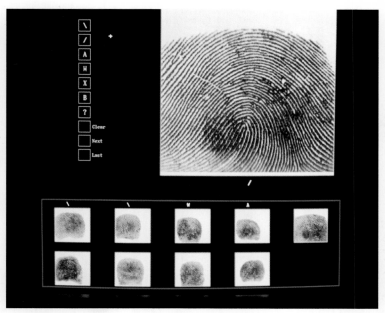

▲ Police share fingerprint information and files across the world. This information helps catch criminals.

CHAPTER 2

TRACE EVIDENCE

Every time you sit on a couch or walk on a rug, you pick up **fibers** (FY-berz). These tiny pieces of fabric stick to your clothes. Fibers also stick to your shoes and skin.

You pick up dirt and grass when you walk across a lawn. You also leave behind hairs and fibers from your clothes. At a crime scene, these things are clues. They are trace evidence.

Police carefully search for trace evidence. They bring it to a lab. Scientists there can prove if a hair or a fiber came from a suspect. This will show if the suspect was at the crime scene.

It's a Fact

Every hour, about three or four hairs fall from your head.

▲ This scientist is looking for trace evidence.

12

TRACE EVIDENCE IN ACTION

Pollen, soil, glass, hair, and fibers are trace evidence.

Here is how someone might leave trace evidence during a crime.

A man walks by a tree. The tree is covered with pollen. The pollen sticks to his jacket. His shoes pick up soil. He enters a house through a broken window. Tiny pieces of broken glass stick to his pants. A hair falls from his head onto the carpet. He sits on a chair. He picks up fibers from the fabric. He leaves fibers from his pants. He leaves pollen from his jacket.

▲ Scientists must be able to analyze the trace evidence. This is a microscopic view of cotton fibers.

Forensic scientists can use each clue to prove that the man was at the crime scene.

EVERYDAY SCIENCE

Under a microscope, the hairs on your head look different than hairs from other parts of your body. Armpit hairs are oval. Head hairs are round. Eyelashes come to a point at the end.

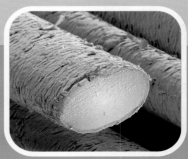

▲ human hair

LOOKING FOR TINY CLUES

Police need patience to collect trace evidence. Police often use tweezers. They must pick up tiny hairs, fibers, paint chips, and more. They carefully save the evidence.

Back in the lab, scientists study every tiny clue. They use many tools to find out what the clues can tell them.

▲ It is important that trace evidence be carefully collected.

SPECIAL TOOLS

A gas chromatograph (kroh-MA-tuh-graf), or GC, is a useful tool. This machine tells what chemicals are in trace evidence.

First, the GC heats the solid piece of evidence. The solid becomes a liquid. Then it becomes a gas. The GC pushes the gas through a tube. The tube separates each chemical in the gas. If two samples have the same chemicals, the samples probably came from the same place.

Another helpful tool is a comparison (kum-PAIR-ih-sun) microscope. Scientists use this tool to look at two things side by side. Scientists may use it to compare two hairs. They use this tool to see if the hairs match.

▲ Modern technology helps police in their work. This is a gas chromatograph.

THEY MADE A DIFFERENCE

Edmond Locard was born in 1877 in France. As a boy, he loved mysteries. Later, he had the idea that "every contact leaves a trace." He meant that criminals always leave trace evidence. They also pick evidence up at the crime scene. This idea is still used in forensic science today.

BONES

Forensic anthropologists (fuh-REN-zik an-thruh-PAH-luh-jists) study bones. Bones can tell if a person was male or female. Bones may tell a person's age or height. They can show the cause of death. Bones can even show with which hand a person wrote.

Math | Matters

Here's one way to estimate a person's height from his or her bones. Measure the femur, or upper leg bone, in centimeters. Then multiply by 2.38 and add 61.4.

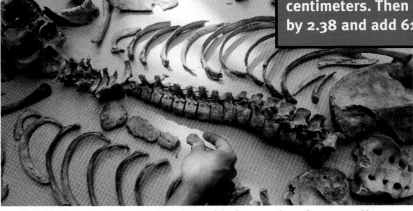

▲ Scientists can gather a lot of information from a pile of bones. One of the first things they do is measure the bones.

The shape and size of a bone are clues. For example, a man's pelvis and jawbone are different from a woman's.

Bones also have marks. When strong muscles are attached to bones, they leave marks. A left-handed person uses the left side more. Those muscles become stronger and mark the bone.

Some bones have breaks or bullet holes. These marks may show how a person died.

Teeth can also give clues. Scientists can use teeth to tell a person's age.

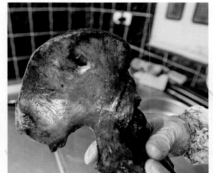

▲ You can see the hole left from a bullet in this human bone.

CAREERS
Forensic Dentist

A forensic dentist studies teeth and teeth marks. Most people get x-rays of their teeth while they are alive. A forensic dentist compares these x-rays to a skeleton's teeth.

Sometimes a criminal leaves teeth marks at a crime scene. For example, he may take a bite of food, leaving the rest. If the bite marks are clear, the forensic dentist can match them to a suspect.

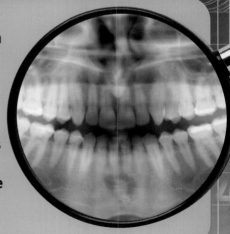

Forensic artists use a person's skull to find out what he or she looked like in life. They look at the bones. Then they make a sculpture or drawing. Detectives use the art to identify the person.

Karen T. Taylor has been a forensic artist for more than twenty years. She has done hundreds of drawings and sculptures of crime victims and criminals. Taylor teaches at the FBI Academy. She also wrote a textbook on forensic art. Here's what she had to say about her job.

Question: What are some methods you use to make a drawing or sculpture from a skull?

Karen T. Taylor: First I gather all the scientific information. A forensic artist works with forensic dentists, police detectives, forensic anthropologists, and other scientists. I include everything from the crime scene, such as hair, a necklace, or a hat.

I use math tables that show average tissue depths. Skin is very close to the bones on the forehead, but down by the cheek it's much fatter. I also use formulas. For example, a relaxed mouth is usually as wide as the front six teeth. It's as wide as eight to ten teeth if a person is smiling.

Question: What would you tell students who are interested in forensic art?

Karen T. Taylor: I would tell them that it's not just about art. It's art and a lot of science.

8446018297398723294

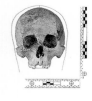  

▲ This forensic scientist is making a reconstruction of a human face.

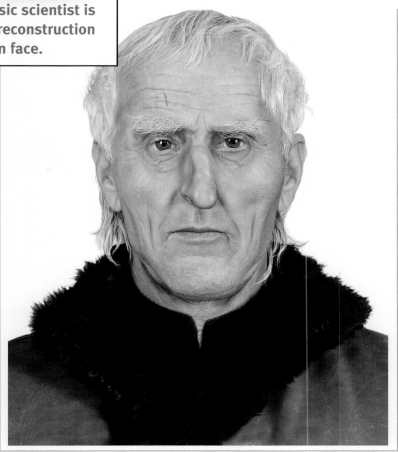

▲ This facial reconstruction was made from a skull that is hundreds of years old.

SHOE PRINTS, TOOLS, AND WEAPONS

Criminals often leave marks at the scene of a crime. Footprints are an important type of mark. Most footprints are actually shoe prints. Police follow shoe prints. Shoe prints can tell about the crime as well as the criminal.

ONE-OF-A-KIND PRINTS

New shoes are difficult to match to a suspect. Many pairs of shoes can be the same brand and size. After someone wears their shoes for a while, the prints become special.

▲ These prints tell more than just a person's shoe size.

 POINT

Talk About It

Sprinkle some soil on the floor. Step in the soil and then on a sheet of white paper. Invite a partner to do the same. Compare the shoe prints. How are they the same? How are they different?

Everyone walks differently. Each person's shoes wear away in different places. Two people can wear the exact same shoes. The prints will still look different.

A worn shoe can crack or become damaged. A pebble may get stuck in the sole. This changes the print.

Police take photographs of footprints at a crime scene. Police may make a **casting** (KAST-ing) of the print. They fill the print with plaster or cement. When dry, the casting is the same shape as the shoe.

It's a Fact

Sometimes detectives need to cast a shoe print made in soft snow. First they spray the print with special wax. The wax hardens. This keeps the print from collapsing when plaster or cement is poured in.

▲ Your shoes may wear at the outside of each heel. Your friend's shoes may wear more at the toe.

BALLISTICS

Ballistics (buh-LIS-tiks). is the study of guns and bullets. Experts use clues from guns and bullets to solve crimes.

All gun barrels have a groove inside. No two guns have the same groove. Even the same type of gun will have different grooves. This is because the tools that are used to make guns wear a little with each use. As a result, every gun barrel is slightly different.

When someone fires a gun, the groove scratches the bullet. Compare two bullets fired from the same gun. You will see that the scratches are the same.

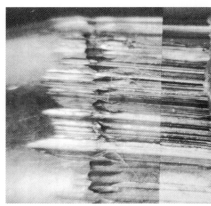

▲ A bullet's groove is as unique as a human fingerprint.

Forensic scientists may want to know if a gun was used in a crime. They must compare two bullets.

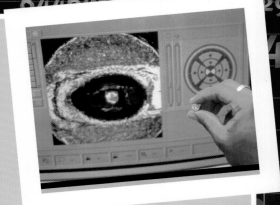

One bullet comes from the crime scene. The second bullet comes from the crime lab. Scientists fire the gun inside the crime lab. They usually fire the gun into a tank of water. This protects the bullet from damage.

A scientist may look at the two bullets side by side.

She may use a comparison microscope. Then she can see if the scratches on the two bullets match.

HISTORICAL PERSPECTIVE   HISTORICAL

The groove in a gun barrel is shaped like a spiral. It makes a bullet spin like a football thrown for a long pass. This helps the bullet travel straight for a long distance. Soldiers in the American Revolution used guns called muskets. Muskets did not have grooves. Muskets were accurate to only about 100 yards (91 meters). Today, guns have grooves.

CHAPTER 4

TOOL MARKS

Criminals use tools to commit crimes. The tools leave marks. These marks may be dents or scrapes.

A criminal may use a screwdriver to open a window. The tool may scrape the wood around the glass.

Forensic scientists look at the size and shape of tool marks. The marks may tell what type of tool was used.

A hammer may leave a dent. Matching the dent to the hammer may be difficult.

Scrapes are easier to match. Tiny chips or bumps in the tool make lines in the scrape. Scientists can look at these lines under a microscope.

▲ By studying these tool marks, scientists may be able to determine what kind of tool made them.

A cutting mark is a tiny ridge on an object that has been cut. Bolt cutters leave cutting marks. Wire cutters leave cutting marks. Knives leave cutting marks, too.

Forensic scientists may look at the edge of a cutting tool. The edge may have trace evidence.

Suppose a criminal used a wire cutter. The criminal cut a wire coated with plastic. Tiny bits of plastic and wire may be stuck to the edge of the tool. Scientists could match the cutting mark to the tool.

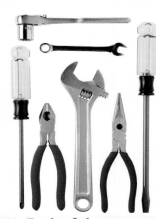

▲ Each of these tools leaves an individual mark.

It's a Fact

Theodore Kaczynski was known as the Unabomber. He sent bombs through the mail that killed and hurt people. He also sent long letters to newspapers about his crimes. Detectives looked at the staples Kaczynski used to fasten the letters. They found marks left by his stapler. These marks were used as evidence against him.

25

DNA

DNA is inside the cells of living things. DNA makes up **genes** (JEENZ). Genes make up chromosomes (KROH-muh-somez). Genes carry instructions that tell cells what to do.

Each person has different DNA. Only identical twins have the same DNA.

Blood and skin are made of cells. These cells have DNA. Saliva has DNA. The root of a hair has DNA, too. Police look for such evidence at crime scenes.

DNA may prove that a suspect is guilty. DNA can also prove that a suspect is innocent.

It's a Fact

Forensic scientists can identify a person's DNA from a tiny amount of blood—less than one drop!

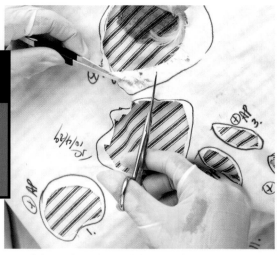

▲ This scientist will use the DNA information in a trial.

DNA Fingerprints

How do scientists use DNA evidence? Here is an example.

Scientists take blood from a crime scene. Then they add chemicals to the blood. The chemicals break down cells. This releases DNA. Then machines make a DNA fingerprint.

A DNA fingerprint is a pattern of short bars. The bars are in long rows.

Experts look carefully at the pattern of DNA from a crime scene. They compare the pattern to a suspect's DNA fingerprint.

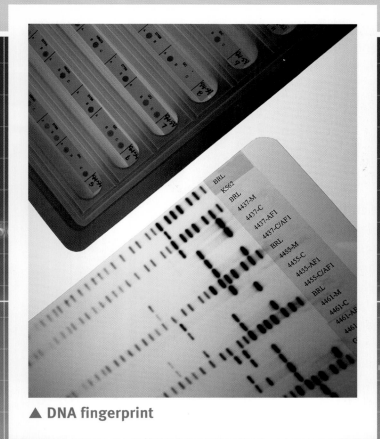

▲ DNA fingerprint

Sometimes police do not have a suspect for a crime. Then scientists will put the DNA fingerprint into a computer.

The computer looks for a match. If a person has gone to jail before, his or her DNA is in the computer.

A DNA fingerprint can lead to clues even if there is no match. For example, it may show if the criminal is related to the victim. Family members share some DNA.

▲ Everyone gets DNA from his or her parents.

CAREERS
Wildlife Detective

Wildlife Detectives try to solve crimes against wildlife. These scientists work with DNA, fibers, blood, guns, and other evidence. For example, police may find meat that they suspect came from an endangered animal. Wildlife detectives test the DNA from the meat to find out for sure.

CONCLUSION

Police once had to solve crimes without science. Today, forensic scientists work all over the world. These scientists help catch criminals and put the criminals in jail.

Scientists find evidence in fingerprints. They look at fibers, hairs, and other trace evidence. They find clues in bones. They look for marks made by shoes, guns, and tools. They use cells to find and match DNA.

Forensic scientists are always finding new ways to solve crimes. What methods do you think these scientists will use one hundred years from now?

☑ POINT

Think About It
Do you think the popularity of television shows and movies about forensic science helps cut down on crime? Why or why not?

CRIME LAB

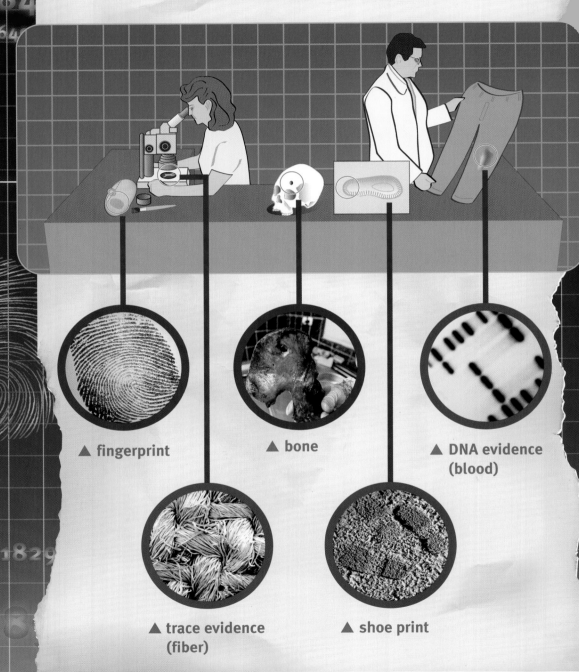

▲ fingerprint

▲ bone

▲ DNA evidence (blood)

▲ trace evidence (fiber)

▲ shoe print

ballistics	(buh-LIS-tiks) the study of guns and bullets to solve crimes (page 22)
casting	(KAST-ing) a form made by pouring plaster or cement into a footprint (page 21)
DNA	(DEE-EN-AY) a substance found in the cells of living things that is unique to each individual (page 3)
fiber	(FY-ber) a tiny bit of fabric (page 12)
fingerprint	(FIN-ger-print) a mark made when a fingertip touches a smooth surface (page 2)
forensic anthropologist	(fuh-REN-zik an-thruh-PAH-luh-jist) a scientist who studies bones to help solve crimes (page 16)
forensic science	(fuh-REN-zik SY-ens) the use of scientific ideas and tools to solve crimes (page 2)
gene	(JEEN) a tiny unit of a chromosome of an animal or plant that determines the characteristics that an offspring inherits from its parent or parents (page 26)
tool mark	(TOOL MARK) a dent or scrape made by a tool during a crime (page 3)
trace evidence	(TRASE EH-vih-dens) tiny pieces of evidence, such as hairs or fibers (page 3)